The Road Ahead

BILL GATES
with Nathan Myhrvold and Peter Rinearson

Level 3

Retold by Donald Domonkos
Series Editors: Andy Hopkins and Jocelyn Potter

Pearson Education Limited
Edinburgh Gate, Harlow,
Essex CM20 2JE, England
and Associated Companies throughout the world.

ISBN 0 582 40211 5

First published in Great Britain by Viking 1995
Published simultaneously in the USA by Viking Penguin
This edition first published 1999
Third impression 1999

Typeset by Digital Type, London
Set in 11/14pt Bembo
Printed in Spain by Mateu Cromo, S.A. Pinto (Madrid)

Published by Pearson Education Limited in association with
Penguin Books Ltd., both companies being subsidiaries of Pearson Plc

Acknowledgements

Pages viii, 5 and 12: Copyright © Alan Fraser (Pennant Illustration);
Page 2: Courtesy of Charles Falco/Science Photo Library; Pages 10
and 28: Illustrations courtesy of Microsoft Press; Page 16:
UPI/Corbis–Bettmann; Page 33: Courtesy of the Lakeside School

Page 20: © 1998 The SABRE Group. Inc. TRAVELOCITY™, the
appearance of TRAVELOCITY Web site, and any other designations are
trademarks of an affiliate of The SABRE Group. Printed with permission.
All rights reserved.

Contents

Introduction

What is a document? Most people will say that it is a piece of paper that tells you something. For more than five hundred years, people have used paper to hold ideas and information. This book is a document.

In fact, a document is anything that tells you something. The news on television is a document, too. There will still be paper in the future, but there will also be other ways to keep and share documents.

New ideas and new ways of doing things. The computer has already changed our lives, and now the world is going to change again because of better, faster communications. How will our lives be in ten years? What will we be doing and seeing? This book is full of questions and answers about the future.

Bill Gates started Microsoft with his friend Paul Allen in 1975, when he was only nineteen years old. It is not a very large company, but Microsoft makes more money than most of the biggest companies in the United States.

Bill Gates was born in Seattle, Washington. He still lives near Seattle with his wife, Melinda.

Nathan Myhrvold has worked at Microsoft since 1986, when it bought a company that he started. Before working at Microsoft, Myhrvold worked at Cambridge University.

Paul Rinearson is a newspaperman and software writer who met Bill Gates in 1982, when he wrote the first important newspaper story on Gates and Microsoft.

Special Words You Will Meet in This Book

These words are in *italics* in the text.

BINARY SYSTEM — The binary system uses "on" and "off" switches to give an alphabet to the computer.

BULLETIN BOARD — You can share ideas with other computer users by sending letters through your computer to a bulletin board. You can read the letters other people have sent.

CABLE TELEVISION — With this kind of television, the pictures that you see don't come through the air; they come through an electric line.

COMPACT DISC — The first compact discs held music. Now they also hold information that you can put into your computer.

COMPUTER SCREEN — The part of your computer that looks like a television. You look at the screen when you are working on the computer.

CONTROL CONSOLE — A control console is a small machine that turns on and off other machines around you.

DATA — Data is another word for information.

ELECTRONIC MAIL (E-MAIL) — Letters that travel through computers are called e-mail.

FILTER — A filter is something in the computer that chooses information for us.

HACKER	– Hackers are people who know a lot about computers and use this to get into other people's computers.
LAPTOP	– A laptop computer is a small computer that you can carry with you.
MICROPROCESSOR CHIP	– The microprocessor chip is the part of the computer that thinks.
PASSWORD	– A password is like an electronic key to open an electronic lock. Only some people know the password and only they can "unlock" the secret information that is in a computer with this "key" word.
SOFTWARE	– Software is the name for the instructions that a computer follows.
TELECOMMUTING	– When you work some place and send your work to another place by using a computer, you are telecommuting. It is a form of communication.
VIRTUAL REALITY	– Computers can use pictures and sounds to make a "place." The place isn't real, but it seems real, and it is possible to think that you are in it.

Chapter 1 The First Part of the Road

I wrote my first program for a computer when I was thirteen years old. A program tells a computer to do something. My program told the computer to play a game. This computer was very big and very slow. It didn't even have a *computer screen*.★ But I thought it was wonderful. I was just a kid, but the computer did everything I told it to do. And even today, that's what I love about computers. When I write a good program, it always works perfectly, every time.

The computer was our toy. We grew up with it. And when we grew up, we brought our toy with us. Now the computer is in our homes and in our offices. It has changed our lives and it is changing them again, because now the computers are coming together to make a new system. In this system, computers all over the world are beginning to work together. Our computers will be our telephones, our post office, our library, and our banks.

When we talk about this new system, we call it the Internet. This book will try to answer questions about the future of the Internet – what it will be like, and how we will use it. Sometimes when we talk about the future of the Internet, we call it the "Information Highway."

◆

The Information Highway, when it comes, is going to bring new ways of doing things. New ways are strange, and sometimes people worry about them, but they are also exciting. I'm very happy that I will be a part of this strange new time.

★You can see the meaning of words with stars next to them in some of the pictures in this book.

I've felt this happiness and excitement before. After I wrote that first program at the age of thirteen, my friend Paul Allen and I spent a lot of time using computers. Back then computers were very expensive. It cost forty dollars an hour to use one. We made some of our money during the summers, when we worked for computer companies.

My friend Paul knew a lot more about the machines than I did. I was more interested in the programs. But I learned from him. One day in 1972, when I was sixteen and he was nineteen, he showed me something that he was reading. It was about a company called Intel that had a new *microprocessor chip*.★

A microprocessor chip is the part of the computer that thinks. This new one wasn't very smart, but we wanted to see if we could write a program for it. In the end, we made a program for it, but we didn't make much money from it.

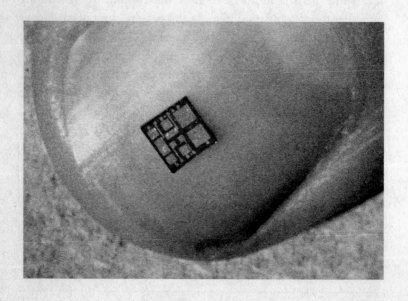

A microprocessor chip.

The next microprocessor from Intel came out in the spring of 1974. It was much smarter than the earlier one. When we read about it, I told Paul that the days of the big computers were finished.

But it was another new idea that excited us more. In December of that year, we saw a picture of the Altair 8800. The Altair was a microcomputer (a small computer) with the new Intel microprocessor chip. When we saw that, we thought "Oh no! People are going to write real programs for this chip!" I was sure of this, and I wanted to be part of it.

It took us five weeks of hard work, but in the end we did it. We had a program for the Altair and we had something more. We had the world's first company that wrote programs for microcomputers. In time we named it "Microsoft."

Starting a company isn't easy. Sometimes it means that you can't do other things that you like. I loved college. I liked having conversations and sharing ideas with so many smart people. But I knew that I had to choose. That spring, Paul decided to leave his job and I decided to leave college. I was nineteen years old.

Chapter 2 Beginnings

To understand the future, it helps to look at the past.

More than a hundred and fifty years ago, a British man named Charles Babbage had an idea about a machine that could work with numbers. He wanted to make a machine that could follow different orders to do different jobs. Today, we call this sort of machine a *computer*, and we call the orders *software*. Software is a group of rules that you can give to a machine to tell it how to do something. Computer programs are software.

For the next hundred years, people worked on Babbage's idea. Finally, in the 1940s, they built the first computer. The United States and Great Britain worked on it together during the war, and the work was secret. Three of the most important men who helped to build it were Alan Turing, Claude Shannon and John Von Neumann.

Even before the war, Claude Shannon was interested in "thinking" machines. He showed how small switches could be the computer's alphabet. In his system, a switch that was off meant "true" and a switch that was on meant "not true." This simple system is called the *binary system*, and computers still use it today.

John Von Neumann, an American born in Hungary, added something just as important. He had an idea about how computers could use a memory in powerful ways. As soon as this was possible, the modern computer was born.

It is not always possible for a computer to keep all its information in its memory without changing it. Often the computer has to make the information smaller so that its memory can hold more of it at one time. Many times it does this before it moves the information to another computer.

Each year we'll be moving more *data*. Data is another word for information. Almost all of the data that we get today in different

4

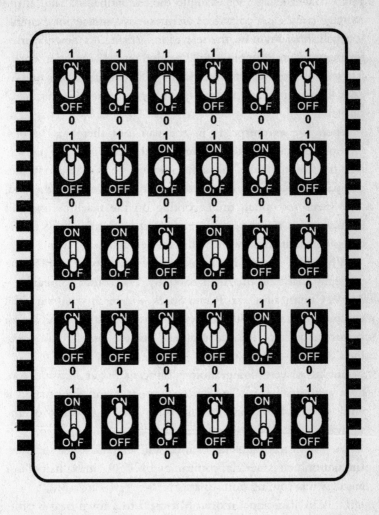

The binary system.

ways will come through our computer, and the computer will send it to different machines around the house. If the computer gets a voice message, for example, the telephone will ring. If the message comes as a picture or pictures – as a movie, for example – it will show them on the television. Writing – a newspaper or fax message, for example – will show up on the computer screen. There will probably be other kinds of information, too, but we can't know yet what it will be, because the future is always full of surprises.

There are no surprises in the past, but there are lessons. Companies that put their money into the Information Highway will try not to make the same mistakes that other computer companies have made during the last twenty years. In the past, they spent too much time working on the machine and not enough time on the software. And they didn't always make computers that could work with other companies' software.

When we started Microsoft, we worked with MITS, the company that built the Altair 8800. By 1977, other companies – Apple, Commodore and Radio Shack – were also making small computers, and we sold them our software. Our software was an important part of these computers, because users could write their programs for it, too.

But users were doing another thing with our software, too; they were stealing it. One person bought it and then shared it with many other computer users by making copies of the software. Sadly, this stealing of software has not disappeared.

Even with this problem, we were still selling a lot of software, and not only to American companies. By 1979, almost half of our business was coming from Japan.

In 1979, Paul and I moved Microsoft to a town near Seattle, Washington. The company was growing. Microsoft was doing so well because we made only software, never computers. The computer companies came to us for the programs. And because almost all of them bought their software from us, our programming language, Microsoft BASIC, was the most important computer programming language.

Computers and their software are different from many other things you buy because they can become more useful. If you buy a computer because you want to play computer games, the computer becomes more useful each time a company makes a new game.

In the beginning, television was not as important in our lives as it is today. At first, there weren't many televisions and so there weren't that many television shows. But as companies sold more televisions, there were more reasons to make more shows. And with more shows, more people wanted to buy televisions.

The same thing happened with *compact disc** music machines. When compact disc machines first arrived in the stores, you couldn't find many of your favorite singers or songs on compact discs. But when enough people began to buy the machines, music companies had to start making more discs. Today, when you want to buy music, you usually buy a compact disc.

These lessons are important for the computer companies. Companies have to remember that people want their computers to do as many different things as possible.

In 1980, two men from IBM came to Microsoft to talk about personal computers, smaller computers that people could use at home or in small businesses. IBM wanted to have these new computers ready in less than a year. It also wanted us to make the software.

IBM's idea seemed wonderful. We wanted to be a part of this. The software system that we made for them was called MS-DOS. We gave them a very low price for using it, and their computers with our software sold very well. Soon other people began to write software that built on top of the MS-DOS system. This was good news for us, because in this way our system became more useful for everyone. For a few years, more than half of all personal computers in business were IBM computers.

The business we did with IBM was very important to us, but in 1992, after some difficulties with different software systems for newer computers, we stopped our work with them.

Nothing that you sell will do well forever unless you work on it and make it better. We made MS-DOS better and better, but in the end we stopped making it. Instead, we sell Microsoft's Windows software. We are planning to make a completely new Windows system every two or three years.

Everyone makes mistakes now and then. What is important is what you do after these mistakes. The secret to winning in our business is change. I believe a company can stay on top by making the right changes at the right time.

Chapter 3 Some Things Computers Can Do for Us

When I was a kid, the Ed Sullivan Show was on television at eight o'clock on Sunday nights. You were in front of the television at eight o'clock or you missed it. And no one wanted to miss the Ed Sullivan Show.

We decide what we watch, but television companies decide when we will watch it. That's the way I watched the Ed Sullivan Show thirty years ago, and that's the way most of us will watch the news tonight.

In the early 1980s, the *VCR*★ began to arrive in homes. The VCR is a machine that makes a copy of movies or TV shows so that you can watch them later or even keep them. Now you can choose when you want to watch something.

Talking on the telephone has changed, too. Before the telephone answering machine, you came home after work and you didn't know that someone wanted to speak with you. Now we can listen to our messages and call people back when we want to.

In the future there will be television as there is now, but there will also be television through the computer. You will be able to watch anything that has already been on TV, at any time you want.

Your mail will also arrive in this way, and the computer will hold it for you until you are ready to read it.

But the Information Highway won't be just a television and a mail-box. It will give us much more. It will help us to learn, to shop, to look after our money, and to talk with our family and friends. It won't matter where in the world they are.

Computer screens will be better than they are now. Their pictures will be clearer, and we will be able to use some of them to write or draw on. Others will work together with the telephone, and will show us the faces of people who are calling us.

9

In today's world, people need to work while traveling. For years we've had the *laptop*,* a small computer that you carry with you, and now there are computers that go in your pocket.

These pocket computers carry information, and they also send letters or play computer games with you. In a few years' time you won't keep money in your pockets, because you'll use your pocket computer to buy things. It will be your little bank, and only you will be able to use it.

One of the problems that people think of when they hear about the future of the Internet is "Too much information." They think that the Internet will be a mountain of data, and that the mountain will fall on them. But "too much information" is not a new problem, and it's not a problem that we only have with computers. Think about books for a minute. When you go to a library, do you worry about reading all the books there? No, of course not. You know what you are interested in. You know what you want to read. And the library system helps you find it.

The Internet has *filters*. A filter helps you choose the information you want. Tomorrow's filters will be better than

A pocket computer.

today's. If you are interested in football, your computer will show you the winners of the football games first when you ask it about sports. Of course, you'll have to tell it things first. The filter will work better if it knows more about you.

Today's computers are like first-day workers. You have to give careful orders about everything. And these computers will always be first-day workers. They cannot learn from you.

A filter that knows a lot about you can learn. It will remember what you're good at. It will remember what you like and don't like. And it will try to help you in other ways.

Because filters will learn, they will also change. When a filter becomes very smart, we call it an "agent." It will even have a voice.

Some people don't like the idea of talking to a computer. "It's too strange," they say. But we talk to machines already. When your car or your computer doesn't work, you shout at it. We shout at things all the time. Now, instead of shouting, we will be able to talk. But most of this won't happen for several years.

Building the future Internet – the Information Highway – will be a big job. The system will have to work with many different kinds of computers and other information machines, too. And it will be expensive to build. But building it has begun already. The Internet is a group of computers that share information. The Internet is already here, and it is the most important new idea in the computer business since the personal computer.

The Internet uses the telephone systems. When I send you a message, it goes from my computer to the telephone, and then from there to my Internet company. Then my company sends it to your Internet company, and your company sends it to you.

The Internet is a wonderful system but it has some problems. One of the most serious problems is *hackers*, people who know a lot about computers and use this to get into other people's computer systems. On November 2, 1988, thousands of computers

Cable television.

using the Internet began to slow down. Many of them just stopped. Companies lost work hours and money. The reason for the trouble was a program that a hacker put into the system several months before.

But most of the time, the Internet works smoothly. Millions of people are using it today, and they are happy with it.

Another change for the Internet is coming, too. Soon you will see movies on your television or on your computer screen because you chose them. These movies will come from *cable television*★ companies. Cable television and telephone companies will fight to get you as a customer for the things they offer: movies, banking, shopping, etc.

The personal computer has helped people in many ways. The Internet will do more; it will open the doors to most of the world's information.

Chapter 4   Changes in Information Systems

What is a document? Most people will say that it is a piece of paper that tells you something. For more than five hundred years, people have used paper to hold ideas and information. This book is a document.

In fact, a document is anything that tells you something. The news on television is a document, too. There will still be paper in future, but there will also be other ways to keep and share documents.

The Internet has let millions of people get to know electronic documents that move from one computer to another. Because computers can do more than paper can, these documents often are more useful to you. The idea of a "document" will change.

When I was young, I loved the encyclopedia that my family had. When I wanted to learn about something, I could read about it and look at pictures of it. I spent a lot of time with the encyclopedia, and I read a lot of it.

Microsoft *Encarta* is an electronic encyclopedia. It has a million words but it also has photographs, movies and music. If you want to know about Egyptian music, you can hear the real music while you read about it. You can also hear what famous people said, or see a movie that explains how a machine works. No paper encyclopedia can give you this.

Paper documents aren't the only ones that will change. The television news will be as long as you want. If you want more information on something they're talking about, you will be able to ask for it.

Already you can share information on the Internet. You can share ideas, too, by putting your letters or messages on a *bulletin board*. An electronic bulletin board is a place in a system of computers where people can read or write messages about something that interests them. A million people can read what you write, or maybe no one will. But either way, you've put your ideas there. And there are bulletin boards about almost everything on the Internet.

Games are another reason people enjoy computers. Today, most computer games are on special compact discs. Every player starts with the same game but he changes it by choosing what he will do with the game. But as the Internet grows, people are beginning to play against other computer users, not just by themselves.

Computers have changed movies, too. It was computer software that gave us the animals in *Jurassic Park* and many exciting parts in other movies like *The Lion King* and *The Mask*.

One of the most interesting ideas in the world of computers is *Virtual Reality*. Virtual Reality, or VR, is a system of pictures and sounds the computer uses to make a "place." The place isn't real, but it seems real, and you think you are in it. You can look to the right and the left, and the system knows that you're turning your head and it changes the pictures. You see these "places" through special computer glasses. With VR, you will be able to learn what it's like to fly an airplane, drive a car, or maybe go inside a body to see the heart working, all without getting out of a chair in your living room.

Today people use a sort of Virtual Reality in many different kinds of computer games, but VR is more than a game. Pilots who are learning to fly airplanes can use it and can "crash" safely, for example. Doctors can use it to practice difficult work.

Virtual Reality systems won't just show us places that we know. There will be wonderful, unreal worlds, too. People are already working to make these interesting, unreal worlds.

Chapter 5 The World of Business

We are leaving the world of paper documents, and because of this, business is changing. The personal computer has already changed how we work, and now that computers are talking to each other business will change even more. The possibilities are exciting, but people have to remember that a computer is only a tool. It can help you with many of your problems, but those problems won't disappear just because you have a computer.

When I was a kid, computers were big machines and only big businesses used them. The computers were part of the reason that these businesses did better than the small ones who used paper and pencil.

One of the first computers in the 1940s.

But today, personal computers have changed all that. Businesses of all sizes use them, and they help their users to do more work.

Today, people in business share information by sending messages and letters, by talking on the telephone and by meeting people from other companies around a table. All of this costs time and money.

At Microsoft, we began to use *electronic mail*, letters that travel through computers, in the early 1980s. e-mail, as everyone calls it, took the place of paper.

e-mail is easy to use and goes from computer to computer immediately. At Microsoft, anyone in the company can send me messages by e-mail. The e-mail messages at Microsoft are usually a sentence or two. The reader gets the information that he needs but it doesn't take as long as a telephone conversation. In the future, e-mail will get better, changing in ways we haven't thought about yet.

Telephones will also get better. You will still hear the other person, but you will also see them, if the other person wants you to. Or you will be able to show other pictures through the same system.

People in business will "meet" without leaving their offices. I'm sure you've already seen people using this sort of communication on news shows on television. People in different countries talk together about the same thing, while a reporter in another place asks them questions. Businesses will find this system useful because it works better than telephone conversations, and it will be cheaper and quicker than bringing people together from around the country or around the world.

There is another part of work that is already changing. In the United States, millions of people work without going to an office every day. They do their jobs at home by using computers, e-mail and fax machines. When you work somewhere and then send your work to another place, you are *telecommuting*. The people who do this are *telecommuters*, and more and more people will be telecommuting in the future, using the Internet.

For this new system of telecommuting to work better, businesses will have to find a new way of thinking about work time. When you are in an office, the company pays you for every hour that you are there. When you are telecommuting from your home, there will be times when you are looking after the baby or doing other things. When this happens, telecommuters will tell their computer, and the computer will tell the office that they are not working at this time.

A lot of companies will become smaller, using telecommuters only when they need them. Big is not always better in business.

Many telecommuters will work for more than one company. They will put their work schedules into the computer, and other businesses will know when they are free to work for them.

Telecommuting will change our lives in many ways. Many of today's problems are problems of the city, of too many people living in the same place because they can find work there.

Of course, there are good things, too, about living in the city. There is more to see and do and the hospitals and schools are bigger and sometimes better. But when people choose to live in the city, they live with the bad so that they can have the good.

Over time, as the Internet brings your work to your home, it will also bring many of the other good things from the city with it: college lessons, city tours, or conversations with doctors at hospital far away. It is possible that when this happens, people will begin to leave the city. It seems strange, but this will possibly help the cities, too. If one person out of ten leaves the city, the city will have more money to spend on the other nine people.

Chapter 6 Markets and Money

When Adam Smith wrote *The Wealth of Nations* in 1776, he talked about a world where every buyer knew every seller's price, and every seller knew how much to ask for.

We do not have that world yet. Sometimes you buy something for $500 and then see it in another store for $300, and you feel stupid. It happens with many different things, but for the same reason. You didn't have enough information.

The Internet will bring buyers and sellers together. You will be able to shop for anything, using your computer. And as this happens, the middlemen, the people who sell things for other people, will have to do more for both the buyers and sellers to keep their jobs.

This idea will frighten a lot of people. But it will stop frightening most of them when it becomes part of our lives. We will ask for more, and get more, from the middlemen.

The travel business is a business of the middleman. The people at the travel office will have to work harder to keep their customers. It will be easy to get travel information through the Internet, and many people will start to plan their own travel.

On the Internet, lots of people will buy things straight from the companies that make them. Because of this, advertising will change. And when you think that something you bought isn't very good, or when you really love it, you'll be able to tell other shoppers about it on the electronic bulletin boards. Before you buy something, you'll be able to read what other people are saying about it on the bulletin boards, too.

Of course, you don't have to listen to everything everyone on a bulletin board says. Sometimes a few users try too hard to tell people how they feel. Their messages become angry. I've seen this happen with bulletin boards, and it kills them.

There's another problem too, with the bulletin boards. Today, if

 If your browser supports SSL encryption, re-enter through our **secure server** now.

Flights

Track down the lowest
fares to anywhere.

Retrieve Existing
Reservations

Don't remember your last
reservations? We do.

Cars

Click through our deals
on wheels.

Hotels

Check in by checking out our
nearly 40,000 hotels.

Vacations & Cruises

Our collection of vacation
packages and cruises will
help make your trip
planning a breeze.

Bed & Breakfasts

Access to more than 20,000
private homestays, bed &
breakfasts and inns from
Inns&Outs.

The Travelocity Customer Service Center will issue and deliver tickets to residents
of the United States and Canada only. Residents outside North America
may purchase and pick up their tickets from a participating SABRE travel agency.

Travel Reservations | Vacations & Cruises | Destination Guide | News & Services

PROFILE - CUSTOMER SERVICE - HELP - TRAVELOCITY HOME

*It will be easy to get travel information through the Internet, and many
people will start to plan their own travel.*

someone keeps telephoning you and you don't want to hear from them, the police and the telephone company will work together to stop them. But no one will get angry at the telephone company. They will get angry at the person who is telephoning.

It's different with newspapers. If a newspaper tells lies about you, the newspaper is in trouble.

The Internet companies are somewhere in the middle, between newspapers and telephone companies. They give us information, but they also bring us information that they didn't write, like the messages on a bulletin board. There have been some problems with the bulletin boards. Some users have become angry at what other users have put there. Does this mean that the Internet company gets into trouble? It isn't clear yet.

I think that, in the end, we will put the information on the Internet into different groups. In some groups, there will be information that the company has read, and changed if necessary. In other groups, the messages will still come straight from other Internet users.

But the bulletin board won't be the only place to find out about things that you want to buy. Today, you can see people in the movies drinking one kind of beer or eating at a restaurant you know. This is a new kind of advertising. In the movie *True Lies*, Arnold Schwarzenegger sees our Windows program in Arabic on a computer screen. We paid for that. In the future, when you see something you like in a movie, you will be able to ask questions about it or even buy it through the computer. If there's a nice hotel in the movie, you'll be able to find out where it is and how much the rooms cost. You'll be able to stop the movie while you do this, and then start it again when you have finished.

Another idea that will change shopping has already started. Levi Strauss & Co is trying a new system for its jeans. At many of its stores, you can tell them how big you want your pants at the stomach and how long your legs are, and their computer sends these numbers to their factory. There, another computer tells the cutting machines, and they make a perfect pair of pants, just for you.

In time, it's possible that everyone will have their personal clothing information in their computer. It will be easier to buy someone a present when this happens. You will know that the clothes will be the right size.

You will also be able to tell your computer about other things you want to buy. Your computer will tell you when it finds something interesting. It will also use this to tell companies about you. This will help both you and the companies.

Advertising today costs companies a lot of money. There are some companies – Coca Cola, for example – who want everyone to see their advertising. But most companies want to get their advertising to one group of people or another. Toy companies want children, or the parents of young children, to see their advertising, for example. Car companies want drivers to see their advertising. And companies that make expensive cars want rich drivers to see their advertising.

When companies know more about you, you won't have to look at advertising for things that don't interest you. And the companies will know that the right people are seeing the things they sell.

Your computer will tell the companies about what you're interested in buying. Or what you're interested in hearing.

Companies that sell music will have new ways of doing business. You will be able to pay for a song each time you listen to it. Or the company will be able to give you a low price for playing it ten times, or maybe you will sometimes be able to play some songs for free. Movie companies will do something like this, too.

There will also be pay-messages. These will give you money if you look at them. Of course, most of these won't give you much money, perhaps a quarter or a dollar. But when someone wants you to notice them specially, you will probably get more. These pay-messages will be another kind of advertising.

Banks will also have to change. There are about 14,000 banks for personal banking in the United States. Most people use a bank near their home or office. But as the Internet becomes better it won't be very important to have your bank near you. There will be electronic banks – computers to watch your money – and these banks will be everywhere because they'll be in your computer, too.

Many companies will have to change when the Internet arrives. Some old jobs will disappear but many new ones will take their place. And buyers and sellers will both win.

Chapter 7 Education in the Future

Businesses will be different, and schools will have to change, too.

Howard Gardner from the Harvard Graduate School of Education says that you have to teach each child in a different way because people see the world differently.

Some teachers are already using the Internet. Many teachers are already using personal computers. In Union City, New Jersey, a telephone company called Bell Atlantic gave 140 computers to students and teachers. These computers went into the homes and the school. At home, children used them to do their homework. Parents used them, too, to talk to the school about their children.

Electronic documents will help teachers to give different parts of the same lesson to different students. All children will learn in the way that is best for them.

A lot of people don't believe this. They have heard about computers in the classroom, but they haven't seen much difference because of them. There is a simple reason for this: money. The schools don't get enough money to buy the right computers. School computers just aren't strong enough and smart enough to do the job. But this will change because it has to change. The computer is in the homes of today, and it will have to be in the schools of tomorrow.

People often ask "Will computers take the place of teachers?" I can answer them, "No, they won't!" A computer is a tool that a teacher uses.

We've all had teachers who made a difference in our lives. But when teachers do great work and give wonderful lessons, they are only helping their 20 or 30 students. In the future, teachers will share their work with other schools across the country, or around the world.

There will be good software programs for the lessons. When a teacher is talking about the sun, for example, she'll be able to choose one of many pictures. She'll have other pictures to show when students ask questions. After the lesson, the students will be able to look for more facts on their computers.

There will be other programs, too, to help the teacher. For each student, she will have a special program with information about that student. Teachers can work better with students and their parents when they know more about the students.

Computers can also help with tests, one of school's most frightening things. Many students are afraid of tests. A student who doesn't do well on tests often starts to be frightened of school in general.

With computers, students will be able to take tests any time, with or without the teacher. When they make a mistake, the computer will help them. Then, when the teacher gives a real test, the students will have a better idea of what they know.

Every school will have a wonderful library, because the Internet will bring millions of books to the school's computer

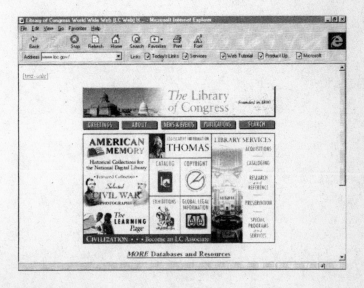

The Internet will bring millions of books to the school's computer screens.

screens. It will also bring electronic documents, like the encyclopedia. Students will be able to ask questions and get answers about almost everything.

Some parents aren't happy when they see their children in front of the computer. "Go read a book," they say. But they are only thinking of computer games. In the future, books will be in the child's computer.

Having all this information isn't the only answer to the problems that many schools have today. But it will help. And our schools are the most important places we have. But there are other places, too, where people need to learn. People everywhere will be able to learn from great teachers, and people of all ages will be able to "go to school" any time they sit down in front of their computer.

Chapter 8 A Home for the Future

Many people believe that computers will take away the time we spend with our friends. Some think that we'll become too comfortable at home and we won't want to leave it. Some think that when we start talking to computers, we'll stop talking to people. I don't believe this.

In the 1950s, people said that movie theaters would die; television will kill them, they said. But movie theaters are still here. People aren't always right.

In fact, the Internet will bring many of our old friends back to us. It will be easier to keep friends who have moved because we will be able to write and talk to them more often and it won't cost as much.

The Internet will help us to make new friends, too. Many of your conversations will start on the computer, but soon you will want to meet.

The Internet will also give you a louder voice in your town or city. If something is making you angry, you'll be able to find other people who feel the same way. Then you will be able to do something together to change the problem, and make your town or city better.

Some parents are afraid of the Internet because it will be a place where their children can learn about anything they want, good or bad. This is a difficult problem.

◆

What comes into the home will be different, but the home will also be different. We won't need many of the things we now have; paper dictionaries and encyclopedias, CDs, the boxes with old letters and old photographs. All this will disappear into the computer. We won't lose them. They will be safe inside our computers. But we will only look at them when we choose.

I'm thinking about all of this because I've recently built a new

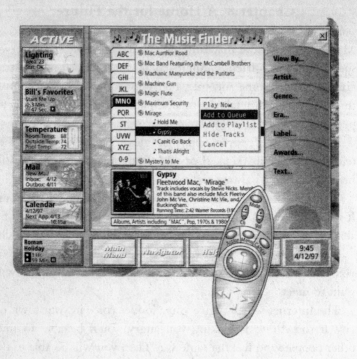

A home control console.

house. My house is a house for the future. It is pretty. But most of all, it is comfortable. It's where my family and I live.

My house is made out of wood, glass and stone. It is also made out of software.

If you come to visit, you'll probably be surprised when you come in. Someone will give you an electronic pin to wear. This pin tells the house who and where you are. The house uses this information to give you what you need. When it's dark outside, the pin turns on the lights nearest you, and then turns them off as you walk away from them. Music moves with you too. If the house knows your favorite music, it plays it. The music seems to be everywhere, but in fact other people in the house hear different music or no music. If you get a telephone call, only the nearest telephone rings.

Of course, you are also able to tell the house if you want something. There is a home *control console*,★ a small machine that turns things on and off around you.

The pin and the console are new ideas, but they are in fact like many things we have today. If you want to go to a movie, you need a ticket. If I give you my car keys, you can use my car. The car works for you because you have the keys. My house works for you because you wear the pin or hold the console.

I believe that ten years from now, most new homes will have the systems that I've put in my house. The systems will probably even be bigger and better than the ones I've put in today.

I like to try new ideas. I know that some of my ideas will work better than others. But I hope that one day I will stop thinking of these systems as new, and ask myself instead, "How did I live without them?"

Chapter 9 The Internet "Gold Rush"

In 1994 and early 1995, when there was a lot of excitement about the Information Highway, it seemed that almost every day one company or another was trying to become part of the plans to build it, to be the first to offer users video through cable television, for example, or video-telephone systems.

It was like an exciting dream – small and large companies hoped to make a lot of money with new electronics and ideas on how to build and run the Highway. Everyone wanted to win. They didn't see much of a place for the personal computer in this picture of the future.

Then, later in 1995, people suddenly seemed to notice the Internet. Communication from one personal computer to another – from office to office, home to home or country to country around the world – was clearly an early move toward a future Information Highway. The excitement over building the Highway turned quickly to excitement over the power that people already had through their personal computers on the Internet. It was a welcome change of thinking for Microsoft, where our thinking and planning was already for "a personal computer on every desk and in every home."

Plans changed fast at every communications, computer and software company. They dropped their ideas for the Information Highway and started to look much more carefully at the "World Wide Web" of personal computers that people were already using. Companies quickly began to make computer hardware and software specially for the Internet, to give users new ways of sending and getting information on almost any subject, of doing business and of making friends, for example.

Internet software is still becoming better and more powerful every day, and in the near future videos and telephone systems will probably run on it, just as people thought when they were making plans for the Information Highway years ago.

The early days of the Internet are like the early days of the California Gold Rush. People will make money in surprising ways.

In 1852, about three years after the start of the Gold Rush, thousands of men hoped to find gold and get rich quickly. A man named Levi Strauss opened a store in San Francisco. Twenty years later, when many people were still dreaming of finding gold, another man from Nevada offered Strauss an idea for a new sort of pants, made of blue "denim." They agreed to go into business together – and they got rich, but it wasn't from gold. Since then the Levi Strauss company has sold more than a billion pairs of blue jeans all over the world – blue gold, we could say.

Almost everybody will some day share in the "riches" of the Internet. It will grow so that almost everyone in the richer countries of the world, and large numbers in the poorer countries, will be users. Microsoft is already working toward that goal.

Chapter 10　Moving into the Information Age

This is an exciting time in the world of computers and information. It is a beginning. New things are coming, and new jobs are coming with them.

I hope for great things from the future, but I worry a little, too. Workers will have to learn these new jobs. Countries will become nearer together, and this will change the way we feel about neighboring countries. There will be new problems, but today we can only guess what they will be.

Sometimes, with everything changing, it seems that the world will be completely different from one day to the next. It won't. But we have to be ready for some changes.

For most people the problem is "Where will my place be in all this?" They worry about their jobs and their children's jobs. These are serious questions. Some jobs will disappear. But these are the same questions I heard when the personal computer arrived in the work-place, and nothing terrible happened then.

Each time a job disappears, the worker who has that job is free to do something new. This means people do more work, and that is good for everyone.

Before we had machines, most people lived or worked on farms. Today, only a few people in the United States do this work. The children and the grandchildren of farmers didn't stop working; they just found new jobs. In 1990, more than half the 501 different jobs you could have were jobs that weren't there in 1940.

Computers frighten almost everyone (everyone but children) before they learn to use them. When people spend more time with computers, they understand them better. You can start by playing computer games or doing other simple things. Once you start using them, I think you'll like them.

The most important users will be today's children and young

1968: Bill Gates (standing) and Paul Allen working at the computer at Lakeside School. You can start by playing computer games or doing other simple things.

people. The Internet is for the future. To give the children this future, we have to do two things. We have to get both girls and boys in front of computers. There are women in the computer business, but there are places for many more. We also have to get the Internet into the schools by giving the schools the lowest price possible for using it.

What will the price of the Internet be? People worry about that. Because the Internet needs as many users as it can get, it will not be expensive.

◆

People are also afraid of sharing too much personal information. Computers already have a lot of information about all of us – the telephone numbers we call, how we did in school or college,

"On the Internet, nobody knows you're a dog."

where we work and how much money we make. Today, these facts are in many different computers. Each computer knows something about you, but no computer knows everything. But the Internet will change that because the computers can all talk to each other. There will have to be new rules for this information: who can see it and how they can use it. We will have to decide on those rules carefully.

At the same time, it's important to remember that computers can also "hide" information. You can keep your information safe by using a secret *password* or number. Computers today have very good systems for this. Computers of the future will have almost perfect systems. Without that password or number, no one will be able to read what's in your computer. Your personal information will be safer, in fact, than ever before.

Yes, there will be problems, but not impossible ones. There will be mistakes, but we will learn from them.

Fifty years ago, Antoine de Saint-Exupéry, a famous French writer and airplane pilot, was talking about the airplane, the telephone and the movies when he said that the best things people have made are all things that bring people together.

The Internet will be a road to many places. I've had an interesting time thinking about some of these places. And I'm excited to be on that road.

ACTIVITIES

Chapters 1–3

Before you read

1 Do you use computers? Why do you use them? What do you like about them? What do you not like?

2 Find these words in your dictionary. They are all in this book. Finish the sentences with a form of these words.

become   copy   future   memory   message   powerful   reason ring   share   show   system   toy

   a Telephones ......

   b Children must learn to ..... things with other people.

   c We know what a computer is now – but what will it .....?

   d Strong people and fast computers are all ......

   e Children play with ......

   f Tomorrow is the ......

   g We use e-mail to send ..... to other businesses.

   h Everything you know is in your ......

   i You can see many new computers at computer ......

   j There are many ..... for Bill Gates' success.

   k I keep a ..... of all my letters.

   l Good ..... make work easier and faster.

After you read

3 Answer these questions.

   a How was the work of these people important to modern computer systems?

   Charles Babbage   Claude Shannon   John Von Neumann

   b What are these?

   the Internet   Microsoft   MS-DOS

4 Talk about this sentence from the book:

   'Our computers will be our telephones, our post office, our library, and our books.'

   Is this true now? How will computers become more useful?

Chapters 4–6

Before you read

5 Bill Gates says, 'The Internet ... will open the doors to most of the world's information.' What problems will there be? What do you think?

6 Answer the questions. Find the new words in your dictionary.
   a Where can you see *advertising*?
   b Name three forms of *communication*.
   c Where do you keep important *documents*?
   d Which machines in your house are *electronic*?
   e What do you look for in an *encyclopedia*?
   f What happens after *life*?

After you read

7 What does Bill Gates say about the future of:
   a television news?   d cities?
   b telephone communication?   e movies?
   c business meetings?

8 Talk about possible uses of the Internet. Which of these is most interesting to you? Why?

   information   e-mail   games   telecommuting   shopping

Chapters 7–10

Before you read

9 Visitors to Bill Gates' home wear an electronic *pin*: 'This pin tells the house who and where you are.' What are the possible reasons for this?

After you read

10 Which of these are Bill Gates' opinions about the future?
   a Children will not need teachers.
   b We will have no time to talk to our friends.
   c We will have fewer paper documents.
   d Many people in poor countries will be part of the World Wide Web.
   e Fewer people will have work.

11 Work in pairs. Talk about one of these subjects:

   families   businesses   countries   friends

   Student A: You think computers will bring people together.

   Student B: You do not agree.

Writing

12 Is *The Road Ahead* a good name for the book? Why (not)?

13 How do you use computers now? How will you use them ten years from now?

14 Describe an electronic house that you would like to live in.

15 Think of a subject that you are interested in. Write a message about it for a bulletin board.